Contents

What is wool?	4
Oily fibres	6
Warm wool	8
Wool colours	10
Wool from sheep	12
Preparing wool	14
Making yarn	16
Knitting and weaving	18
Making patterns	20
Wool for clothes	22
Wool indoors	24
World wool	26
Fact file	28
Would you believe it?	29
Glossary	30
More books to read	32
Index	32

You can find words shown in bold, **like this**, in the Glossary.

What is wool?

Wool is a **natural** material. It comes
from the coats of sheep and some
other animals. This wool grew on
sheep. It has been cut off and is ready
to be used.

Materials

Wool

Chris Oxlade

www.heinemann.co.uk/library
Visit our website to find out more information about **Heinemann Library** books.

To Order:
Phone 44 (0) 1865 888066
Send a fax to 44 (0) 1865 314091
Visit the Heinemann Library Bookshop at www.heinemann.co.uk/library to browse
our catalogue and order online.

First published in Great Britain by Heinemann Library, Halley Court, Jordan Hill, Oxford OX2 8EJ
a division of Reed Educational and Professional Publishing Ltd.
Heinemann is a registered trademark of Reed Educational & Professional Publishing Ltd.

OXFORD MELBOURNE AUCKLAND JOHANNESBURG BLANTYRE
GABORONE IBADAN PORTSMOUTH (NH) USA CHICAGO

Designed by Storeybooks
Originated by Ambassador Litho Ltd.
Printed in Hong Kong / China

ISBN 0 431 12724 7 (hardback)   ISBN 0 431 12731 X (paperback)
05 04 03 02 01   06 05 04 03 02
10 9 8 7 6 5 4 3 2   10 9 8 7 6 5 4 3 2 1

British Library Cataloguing in Publication Data
Oxlade, Chris
Wool. – (Materials)
1. Wool
I. Title
620.1'97

Acknowledgements
Ardea/London p.7; Bruce Coleman Collection /Bob Glover p.12, /Sir Jeremy Grayson p.13, /Gordon
Lansbury p.8; Corbis /James L Amos p.4, /Jacqui Hurst pp.18, 20, /Penny Tweedie p.29, /Science Pictures
Ltd p.6; Elizabeth Whiting Assocs p.24; Impact p.14; Jacqui Hurst p.17; Still Moving /Doug Corrance
pp.16, 21, 27, /Ken Paterson p.11; Trip /J Drew p.26, /J Greenberg p.9, /H Rogers pp.10, 15, 19, 23; Tudor
Photography pp.5, 22, 25.

Cover photograph reproduced with permission of Tudor Photography.

Every effort has been made to contact copyright holders of any material reproduced in this book.
Any omissions will be rectified in subsequent printings if notice is given to the Publisher.

Wool is an important material. It is made into clothes, blankets, carpets and curtains. All the things on this page are made from wool. They are called woollen objects.

Oily fibres

A sheep's **fleece** is made of millions of short, thin pieces of wool called **fibres**. They are like the hairs on your head. This is what the fibres look like through a **microscope**.

The wool fibres in a sheep's fleece are covered in an oily liquid called **lanolin**. The lanolin makes the coat **waterproof**. It stops the sheep's skin getting wet.

Warm wool

Wool is soft and warm to touch. A sheep's coat keeps the sheep warm in the cold. It does this because there is warm air trapped between the wool **fibres**.

Clothes made from wool keep you warm when it is cold. Thick and fluffy woollen hats trap warm air next to your head. A scarf traps warm air around your neck.

Wool colours

Most sheep have white or creamy **fleeces**. Some have brown or black fleeces. Some grow two different colours of wool at the same time.

The wool that we use for clothes and **furnishings** comes in many different colours. This is because we can colour wool using **chemicals** called **dyes**.

Wool from sheep

Farmers cut the sheep's long, woolly **fleece** off with large scissors called shears, or electric clippers. This is called sheep shearing. Like a haircut, it does not hurt!

Sheep are sheared at the beginning of summer, when the weather gets warmer and the sheep don't need their fleeces. The fleeces grow back again in time for winter.

Preparing wool

The wool in a **fleece** that has just been sheared is oily with **lanolin**. It is also dirty and tangled up. So it is washed in **detergent** to get the lanolin and dirt off.

After being washed, the wool **fibres** are untangled by a special machine. It combs the wool with stiff wire brushes. This is called carding.

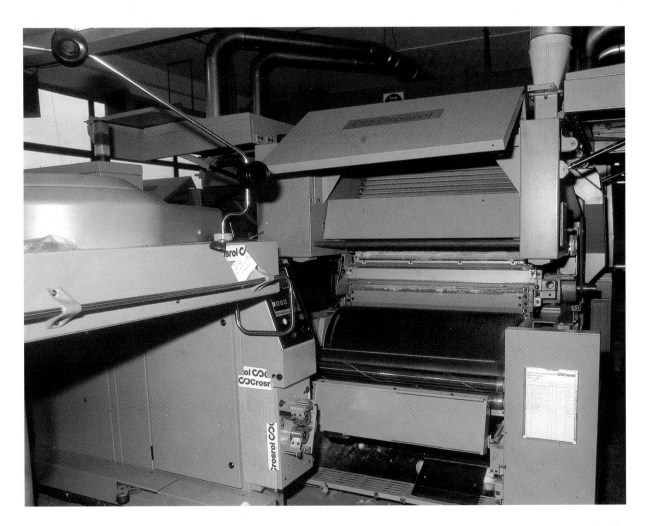

Making yarn

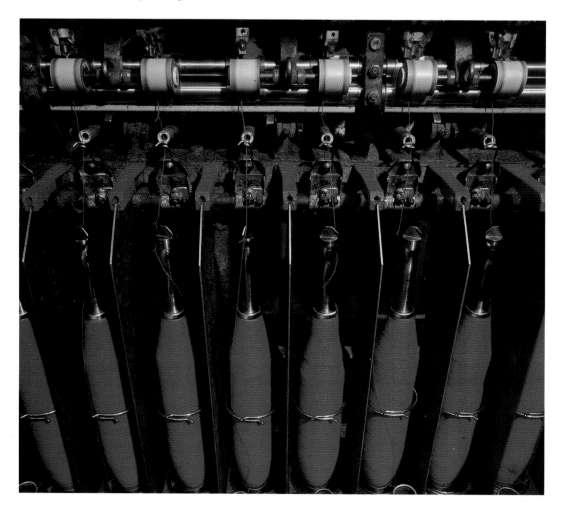

This wool is being made into a long, thick string called yarn. To make yarn, the short wool **fibres** are twisted together. Wool yarn is easy to pull apart.

Yarn can be made stronger and thicker by twisting two yarns together. This is called two-ply yarn. Now the wool is ready to be made into fabrics.

Knitting and weaving

Woollen **yarns** are made into fabrics by **knitting** or **weaving**. The knitter knits fabric by making small loops of yarn with knitting needles. Knitting is also done on knitting machines.

Weaving is done by a machine called a **loom**. The machine weaves some pieces of yarn over and under other pieces of yarn to make fabric.

Making patterns

Knitted and woven fabrics can have beautiful patterns in them. The patterns can be made by **knitting** or **weaving yarns** of different colours together.

Patterns can also be made by weaving yarns in different ways. The pattern in this cloth is called herringbone. **Looms** can **automatically** weave different patterns.

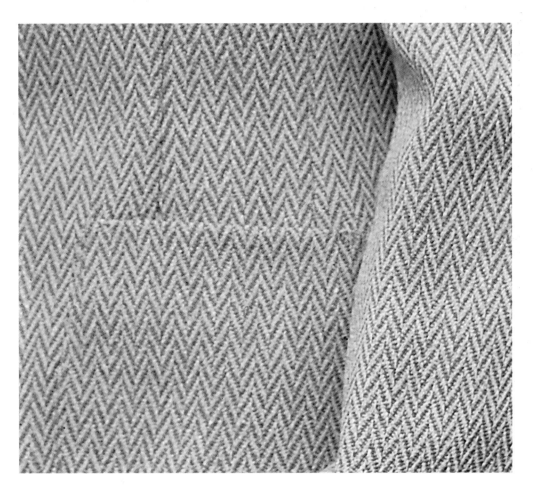

Wool for clothes

Many different clothes are made from wool. Warm woollen clothes such as jumpers are knitted or woven with thick two-ply or three-ply **yarns**.

Lightweight woollen clothes such as smart jackets are made from thin, smooth fabrics. The fabrics are knitted or woven with thin, soft yarns. They are still quite warm.

Wool indoors

You can see woollen fabrics in homes, too. Sofas and chairs are often covered in woollen fabrics. Cushion covers can also be made from wool.

Wool carpets and rugs are soft and warm to walk on. People have made rugs and carpets from wool for thousands of years. They often have colourful patterns in them.

World wool

Most wool used in the world comes from sheep. But some wool comes from the coats of other animals. In South America, people make fabrics with wool from these animals called alpacas.

Cashmere is a type of wool that comes from Kashmir goats. Cashmere wool is very smooth and soft, but expensive. It is made into smart clothes such as cashmere sweaters.

Fact file

▶ Wool is a **natural** material. Most wool comes from the coats of sheep.

▶ Wool is soft and warm to touch.

▶ Wool on a sheep is **waterproof** because it has **lanolin** in it.

▶ Natural wool is white, creamy, brown or black. Wool can be coloured with **dyes**.

▶ Wool is made stronger by twisting it into **yarn**.

▶ The wool from some sheep is softer than the wool from other sheep.

▶ Electricity does not flow through wool.

▶ Wool is not attracted by **magnets**.

Would you believe it?

Most wool comes from Australia. There are about 200 million sheep in Australia. That is ten sheep for every person who lives in Australia!

Glossary

automatically   on its own, without a person working it

chemicals   special materials that are used in factories and homes to do many jobs, including cleaning and protecting

detergent   chemical that cleans the dirt from fibres and fabrics

dye   substance that colours fibres and fabrics

fibre   thin thread, or tiny piece, of material. Wool is made of fibres.

fleece   woolly coat of a sheep

furnishings   furniture and decorations in a home, such as sofas, carpets, curtains, tables and chairs

knitting   making fabric with small loops of yarn joined to each other

lanolin oily liquid on the wool of a sheep's fleece

loom machine that weaves fabrics from yarns

magnet object that pulls steel and iron objects towards it

microscope device that makes things look bigger than they are. It is used to look closely at things.

natural comes from plants, animals or the rocks in the earth

waterproof does not let water in or out

weaving making fabric by putting yarns over and under each other

yarn long string of material made by twisting fibres together

More books to read

Farm Animals: Sheep
Rachael Bell
Heinemann Library, 1999

Images: Clothes
Karen Bryant-Mole
Heinemann Library, 1997

Look Around You: The Clothes We Wear
Sally Hewitt and Jane Rowe
Evans Books

Working Worldwide: Farmers
Jane Shuter
Heinemann Library, 1997

Images: On the Farm
Karen Bryant-Mole
Heinemann Library, 1997

Images: Materials
Karen Bryant-Mole
Heinemann Library, 1996

Index

alpaca wool 26
carding 15
carpets 5, 25
cashmere wool 27
chemicals 11
clothes 5, 9, 11, 22–23
dyes 11, 28
fibres 6, 8, 15, 16
fleece 6, 7, 10, 12, 13, 14

furnishings 11
knitting 18, 20
lanolin 7, 14, 28
shearing 12, 13
sheep 4, 6, 7, 8, 10, 12, 13, 26, 28
weaving 18, 19, 20, 21
yarn 16–17, 18, 19, 20, 21, 22, 23, 28